CLOSING TIME

The 7 Immutable Laws
of Sales Negotiation

This book is dedicated to Stan and Blanche Hubsher,
two of the most special and inspirational
people I know.

CLOSING TIME

The 7 Immutable Laws
of Sales Negotiation

Ron Hubsher
CEO, Sales Optimization Group

Praise for our Sales Negotiation System and Book

"This is a well thought out, repeatable system to close sales, increase the lifetime value of clients, eliminate discounting, and enhance brand equity. It is filled with immediately actionable steps to increase margins and profitability on your very next deal. It is one of the most profitable and valuable business books you can read."

— Ray Lane: Managing Partner: Kleiner, Perkins, Caufield & Byers, former President and COO of Oracle Corporation

"An outstanding system for negotiating and closing sales opportunities on a global basis. I would recommend it to executives looking to drive revenues, command price premiums, and increase shareholder value. It is easy to understand, easy to use, and easy to implement. It is a must read."

— Jim Steele: Chief Customer Officer, Salesforce.com

"This is an essential read for the career of anyone in the profession of sales or sales management. It demystifies the sales negotiation process and helps close more sales with little or no discount. I highly recommend this book and system."

— Mary Delaney: Chief Sales Officer, CareerBuilder

"Ron has created a straightforward, easy-to-implement system for negotiating and closing sales opportunities. It is an excellent process for executives seeking to increase margins, improve close rates, and accelerate revenue growth."

— David Berman: President, Worldwide Sales Webex/Cisco

"**I have read countless books on negotiating skills over the years, but Closing Time is the first I've seen that is written specifically for sales negotiation.** Sales negotiations are uniquely challenging, and this book provides easy-to-use strategies that help overcome those unique challenges to closing deals and enjoying price premiums over competitors. It might just lead to the end of discounting."

— *Todd Johnson, Chief Marketing Officer, Verisign*

"**This is a no-nonsense, action-oriented book on sales negotiations that draws on Ron's intensive experience in this field.** Read it in the morning, and by the afternoon you'll be more effective in closing more deals and generating more revenue."

— *Kamel Jedidi: Chairman of Marketing Department: Columbia Business School*

"**It's a splendid work; tight, actionable and realistic.** And, unlike most books on negotiation, it has simplicity without being simplistic and wisdom without preaching. But the best thing about *Closing Time* is its sales orientation. This isn't a warmed over repeat of the Harvard Negotiation Project, or a treatise on games theory. It is practical sales advice on maintaining and improving margins – and it's sorely needed in most sales forces."

— *Neil Rackham: Author, SPIN Selling*

"**This is a great business book. It is a quick read and provides very practical advice** on how to optimize selling and relationship building. I've already put some of the "immutable laws' into effect and I am giving everyone on my team a copy."

— *Gil Irwin: Senior Partner, Booz Allen Hamilton*

"This is the best book I have ever read on Sales Negotiation.
It provides readers with real-world tools and a system to negotiate
and close profitable sales and increase brand equity. It is an essential
read for any sales executive and has created a new standard for sales
negotiation that works worldwide."

— *Bob Bakish: President, MTV Networks International*

"In his book, Ron shares his unique, practical perspectives
on increasing and closing rates, securing better, higher margin
agreements, and increasing lifetime value of prospects and clients."

— *Mike Katz: Senior Executive Advisor & Retired Sr. Partner,
Booz Allen & Hamilton*

**"*Closing Time* presents clear, practical guidance for one
of the most vexing business challenges** faced by entrepreneurs:
negotiating and closing sales. Touching on discounts, relationships
and research, this short book should serve as a handy best-practices
guide for owners, sales managers, and investors."

— *Karen E. Klein, Business Columnist, BusinessWeek*

"*Closing Time* is an invaluable tool in any business. Ron's
easy-to-use and easy-to-implement negotiation system, which
fosters development of buyers with a greater lifetime value, encourages better client relationships and agreements, while growing top
line revenue and driving bottom line profitability. For the one book
your team should read, Closing Time should be your choice. I highly
recommend it!"

— *Carol E. Robbins: Chief Branding Officer, Prudential Financial, Inc.*

"*Closing Time* should be required reading for not only sales personnel but the entire management team.** Ron provides a clear, simple, and practical sales and negotiation framework that the entire organization can embrace."

— *Ira B. Polikoff, Senior Vice President & Lead Financial Officer, American Express Global Network Services*

"As a consultant, researcher, and salesperson, I have observed some of the best and worst sales negotiations of all time. *Closing Time* **reveals the best practices that I have seen used by top salespeople and negotiators around the world.**"

— *Jason Jordan: Principal, Mercer Sales Effectiveness Consulting*

"This is a great system for any executive with revenue responsibility. Closing Time provides a practical, repeatable negotiation process that focuses on value rather than discounts, creates better agreements between sellers and buyers, and strengthens client relationships. It is a great investment of time and offers a new approach to negotiation."

— *Scott Schulman, President, Dow Jones Financial Information Services*

"This is the gold standard for negotiating and closing sales. It will help you reduce discounting and increase close rates the very next day."

— *Gerhard Gschwandtner: Founder and Publisher of SellingPower Magazine*

"Ron brings his sales experience to the negotiating portion of the sales process so that it is not a disconnected, theoretical—or worse, irrelevant—exercise. The skills and techniques he's refined in his years of consulting and training are now presented clearly and concisely in Closing Time. Read it now to improve your sales and business results!"

— *Barry Trailer: CEO CSO Insights: Former President of Miller Heiman*

"There are only four "Bottom Line" criteria for a business book to become a classic:

1. it's easily readable;

2. it cuts right to the chase with straightforward unambiguous steps;

3. it's intuitively obvious once you recognize the process;

4. it's easy to remember and start using Monday morning.

This should be a classic!"

— *Howard Stevens: CEO, H R Chally, Author of "Achieve Sales Excellence"*

"Ron repositions the negotiation process as a true partnership. His solid advice will show you how to win new high margin business, grow your top line, dramatically increase your profits, and become vitally important to your clients."

— *Patrick Sweeney: Executive Vice President, Caliper Inc., Author of the New York Times bestseller "Succeed on Your Own Term"*

"**What makes *Closing Time* such an important book is that it explores the financial impact that effective negotiation will have on your business.** Once you see the numbers, you'll be compelled to follow Ron's advice."

— *Dave Stein: CEO and Founder, ES Research Group, Inc.*

"***Closing Time* offers a consistent, repeatable process to close sales opportunities and increase margins.** It is easy to implement and easy to use. It makes negotiation a science that creates eager and satisfied buyers who will become long term profitable customers. In short, it is an excellent system."

— *Ken Nordine: Chairman of Sales Leadership Roundtable: University of Chicago, Graduate School of Business*

"***Closing Time* is an easy to use system that helps you create better agreements and improve client relationships.** It is a great system for anyone looking to enhance their business."

— *Nadine Wong, Executive Director, Morgan Stanley Private Wealth Management*

"***Closing Time* is a book that is incredibly thoughtful and extremely practical.** It provides the reader with the necessary tools and techniques for successful sales negotiations. It must be a part of every executive's business library and every sales person's key competency. I heartily endorse it."

—*Steve Gasten: Former President, Holden International*

Want to get your team trained?

Our customized training programs range from 1 hour to 1 day. Payback is usually achieved in a matter of days.

We serve clients worldwide.

If you would like to get your team trained, please call us at:

650-520-9849

Contents

Introduction

ABOUT THIS BOOK

This book is designed to help you negotiate and close competitive sales opportunities. It is based on the Sales Optimization Group's work with world-class sales organizations involved in the sales of high-value products and services. The book is based on our proven, patent-pending system that is on file with the United States Patent and Trademark Office. These **"7 Immutable Laws"** have been used worldwide with great success. I am grateful that you have selected this book and I look forward to hearing your success stories.

You should read this book if:

You are a CEO, CFO, CSO, or business owner who is looking to geometrically improve profitability and market valuation, increase the lifetime value of clients, and better serve customers and prospects.

You are a CSO, VP of sales, or sales manager looking to meet your forecast, increase close rates, accelerate the sales cycle, command price premiums, reduce discounting, and reduce the amount of time and effort it takes to negotiate and close sales.

You are a salesperson interested in closing more sales more quickly and making more money without having to work harder. In fact, reading this book and applying its principles will enable you to free up more time for your personal life or time to invest in making more sales and more money.

You are an investor who is looking to make extraordinary returns by increasing sales performance and market valuation for shareholders.

What you will learn

By putting sales negotiation best practices into place, you will learn how to:

- improve your negotiation strategy and execution;
- reduce or completely eliminate discounting and command price premiums;
- negotiate better agreements that expand the pie for both parties;
- create and develop buyers with larger lifetime value;
- increase close rates and reduce the number of stalled sales opportunities;
- accelerate sales velocity, shorten the sales cycle, and close more sales;
- geometrically increase market valuation; and
- make negotiation one of your core assets and a key strategic competitive advantage.

Best of all, there is nothing theoretical about the laws in this book. Every one of them can be easily and effectively implemented tomorrow.

What makes this book different from other negotiation books?

This book focuses on sales negotiation specifically and is uniquely designed from proven successful laws that help close sales opportunities. Many books on negotiation focus on how to settle or resolve disputes between two parties who are forced to deal with each other. For example, they describe how a company can resolve a dispute with a labor union. They may cite how they helped one country resolve a conflict with another. They may talk about how a manager should negotiate with an employee. In each of these situations, the common factor is that each side must deal with the other side: neither side can simply walk away from the situation and neither side has an easy alternative. If the parties do not reach some agreement, each side will face consequences and repercussions from the other. Often, the two sides will use these negative consequences as leverage to create a middle ground—one that is less than fantastic for either party. However, since there is no easy alternative—as there is in a sales situation where there is at least one competitor waiting in the wings—it is better to reach agreement than to suffer the prolonged consequences of no agreement, and to come to an agreement that is marginally better than not coming to an agreement at all. With the best of intentions, many of these books try a one-size-fits-all approach and try to extend these concepts to sales. Unfortunately, these concepts fail miserably in sales situations. It is like trying to fit a square peg in a round hole.

In other words, it's just not applicable.

What makes sales negotiation different from other types of negotiation?

- Sales negotiation is not conflict resolution. It is about co-creating a great agreement that allows the seller and buyer to create a great relationship, not creating a marginally better agreement based on fear and reprisals.

- In sales negotiation, the buyer may opt to do nothing. "Buyers" are not forced to buy from you. They may simply choose to take no action and keep the status quo.

- The buyer may choose to select one of your competitors with a similar offering and choose never to do business with you. In fact, most of the time you will be competing against a number of qualified competitors.

- The buyer may decide not to negotiate with you at any time for any reason and suffer no adverse consequences or repercussions.

- Buyers will rarely agree to a sale that makes them marginally better. It's just not worth the effort and risk. The sale has to meet financial hurdle rates that work for the buyer and make the buyer much better off.

It is precisely for these reasons (and due to the fact that competitors are always waiting in the wings vying for the same business you want) that sales negotiation is a different and more complex process, one that requires a different kind of approach. It is also why these **7 Immutable Laws** are so valuable.

In essence, this book speaks to the needs of a sales negotiator because:

- It is designed exclusively for sales negotiation;

- It is particularly effective for complex business-to-business sales and sales of high-value/high-risk products and services;

- It reveals **Action Items** at the end of each section that are easy to implement;

- Its methods have been proven successful for closing sales worldwide; and

- It is a practical guide with practical strategies and tools you can implement easily and effectively.

I thank you for selecting this book and investing your time.

ABOUT THE AUTHOR

Ron Hubsher is CEO of the Sales Optimization Group (www.salesog.com), an international sales and negotiation training and consulting organization. The company assists clients in financial services, technology, business & professional services, media and manufacturing to accelerate sales through use of its patent pending sales and negotiation processes, methodologies and tools. Some of its clients include **Google, Oracle, ADP, Adobe, Prudential, Morgan Stanley, Walgreens, Kimberly-Clark, Comcast, Thomson Reuters, Sun Microsystems, Sprint, the Columbia Business School** and many others.

Ron has over 25 years of sales, sales negotiation, and sales management experience. Mr. Hubsher is the architect of numerous proven processes and methodologies to optimize and accelerate sales and negotiation results. Many of his processes and methodologies, including those in this book, are on file with the United States Patent and Trademark Office.

He is a sought-after speaker and is regularly asked to participate, contribute, present, and share his sales and negotiation thought leadership at many conferences and with many publications. These include **BusinessWeek,** the **LA Times, Inc. Magazine, Selling Power Magazine,** the American Marketing Association, the Columbia Business School Alumni Association, the Wharton Alumni Association, the University of Chicago Graduate School of Business Sales Leadership Roundtable, the National Association of Small Business Investment Companies, the Columbia Business School Executive MBA Speaker Series, the Indus Enterprise, Marketing Executives Network Group, Webex, CRM Radio, CRM Guru and others.

Prior to leading the Sales Optimization Group, Mr. Hubsher was in sales management at a leading on-demand CRM provider, UpShot (acquired by Siebel, subsequently acquired by Oracle), where he helped many world-class companies accelerate sales and negotiation performance. A former management consultant with Booz, Allen & Hamilton, Mr. Hubsher has worked with and provided thought leadership for Fortune 500 companies on their sales, sales negotiation and business strategies.

Mr. Hubsher holds an MBA from Columbia Business School and a Bachelor of Science degree in Operations Research from Columbia University.

Editor's Note: You will probably notice that we use the pronoun "he" when speaking about buyers and salespeople. We did this to keep this book easy to read. We apologize if this offends our readers in any way. It is in no way meant to preclude or exclude the many spectacular women who are part the sales profession and are integral leaders of today's business world. We use the singular pronoun "he", "his", and "buyer" to refer to your customers and prospects. In fact, you will find that often there will be multiple decision makers and influencers with whom you negotiate and engage in the course of sales negotiation. Again, this is done for readability's sake alone.

Section I

Sales Negotiation

Chapter 1
The Strategic Importance of Sales Negotiation

Your sales negotiation strategy and execution has a huge effect on your business. Your sales negotiation strategy and plan dramatically influence your net income and market valuation. They also have a dramatic impact on the success of your sales team and directly impact how your customers and prospects view you. Despite this huge impact, however, less than 5% of companies have a well-articulated negotiation strategy and even fewer have an effective plan to execute it. When a company and a salesperson offer a discount to close business or to attempt to close business, this decision creates a rippling and crippling effect for the business. Contrary to the belief that they are winning business, they have set the seeds for a series of bad events, including reduced corporate profits and market valuation. Let's take a deeper look at the dramatic impact the absence of a negotiation strategy can have, and the upside potential that is available to you as soon as you start implementing the **7 Immutable Laws**.

1. Poor sales negotiation strategy and discounting have a geometrically devastating impact on net income and market valuation. Many companies, including public ones, have net incomes in the range of 8% to 15% as a percentage of their sales. These same companies often discount 10%, 20%, and 30%. They are geometrically hurting their net income, market valuation, and prospects for future success.

If you are an investor, CEO, or VP of sales, you now have the opportunity to capitalize on the huge upside potential to immediately and dramatically impact market valuation and net income by putting the **7 Immutable Laws** to work for you. (See Figure 1)

In Figure 1, we've analyzed one such public company with sales of $2.516 billion and a net income of $226 million (9% of sales). The company's current price/earnings ratio is 18 and its market valuation is $4.076 billion ($226 million x 18).

If discounting could be reduced by 10%, the company's net income would increase to $390 million and its market valuation would increase to $7.020 billion. Thus, a 10% reduction in discounting would lead to a 72% increase in net income and market valuation, and would generate a large creation of income and market valuation for employees and shareholders.

If discounting were reduced by 20%, the company's net income would increase to $554 million and its market valuation to $9.963 billion. Thus, a 20% reduction in discounting would lead to a 144% increase in net income and market valuation—more than double its current net income and market valuation.

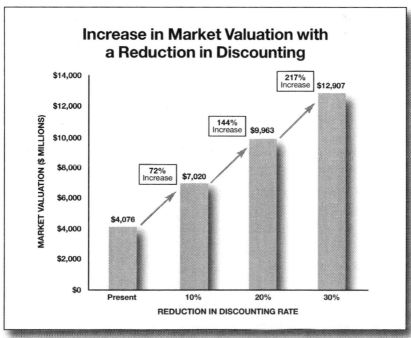

Figure 1

If discounting were reduced by 30%, the company's net income would increase to $717 million and its market valuation to $12.907 billion. Thus, a 30% reduction in discounting would lead to a 217% increase in net income and market valuation—more than *triple* its current net income and market valuation.

NOTE: This calculation does not include the effect on close rates when you implement a negotiation strategy and implement the **7 Immutable Laws**. If you do, these numbers become even more dramatic!

Your ability to implement a negotiation strategy can have a huge impact on the financial health of the company and offers you an opportunity to increase your sales, net income, and market valuation.

2. Your sales negotiation strategy reaches far beyond the numbers. Your negotiation strategy not only affects net income and market valuation, but has more far-reaching implications. It impacts your ability to raise capital, your ability to attract and retain key people, your ability to reward employees, your ability to invest in research and development, your ability to enter new markets, your ability to launch new products, and your ability to market and create demand. In Figure 1, which organization would *you* rather be? Discounting causes a negative corporate spiral. The less you discount the stronger your prospects for continued and ongoing success.

A strong negotiation strategy causes a consistent upward corporate spiral.

3. An inconsistent sales negotiation strategy and discounting creates a hidden corporate liability. What happens when you sell with a different discount level across territories? For example, suppose your customer Company X gets a 10% discount in Hong Kong, a 30% discount in Los Angeles, a 20% discount in New York City, and a 40% discount in London. Or suppose Company X acquires Company Y, and Company Y gets a 50% discount. What happens then? It may not happen immediately, but eventually your buyer is going to figure it out and when he does, watch out. Not only can you be assured that the VP of sales, CEO, CFO, or some other executive is going to have a very challenging conversation, but also that some likely concessions are going to be made to your customer that adversely affect your profitability. When you don't have a negotiation strategy, this liability continues to grow.

A cohesive negotiation strategy helps you eliminate this corporate liability.

4. Discounting creates a legacy and reduces the lifetime value of a customer. If you complete a sale with a discount, what happens the next time your customer wants to do more business with you? Is he going to accept your full asking price? Not likely. What is he going to expect? At the very least, your last discount. So if your last discount was 20%, he will probably accept no less on a future sale. In fact, the 20% discount might be the starting point for negotiations in future sales. Not a pretty picture, is it? Poor negotiation and discounting creates a legacy that severely reduces the lifetime value of your customer.

An effective negotiation strategy and plan helps you increase the lifetime value of your customers.

5. Discounting erodes brand equity and corporate credibility. How do you feel about a person or a company that tries to fool you or does not tell you the truth? Probably not very good. In the case where you are the salesperson, you have gone through a long, in-depth sales cycle. You have proven that you are the best solution. You have proven that your company is credible and ethical, that you are experts, and that your company offers unique value. You have tried to earn the trust of all the key decision makers and you have shown them that they will lower their personal risk by selecting your company as the best vendor. So what happens next? You offer them an inflated price that is not the real price. You give them a price you were hoping they would be foolish enough to accept.

What does that say about you? What does that say about your credibility? They may infer that you have not dealt with them in an upfront and honest manner. They may wonder in what other ways you may have tried to take advantage of them. What other terms and conditions are you trying to slip by them? What other liberties have you taken during the sales cycle? Where else have you put fat into the agreement? Your credibility may get called into question. The more you discount the more you erode your credibility.

Is this the way you want to start a relationship? Is this how you want your company to be perceived? Is this behavior congruent with the years it took to build your company, the investment you have made to create your products and services, the investments you have made to build your brand?

A strong negotiation strategy enhances your brand equity and enhances your corporate credibility.

6. Poor sales negotiation skills and discounts in one sales opportunity impact other (seemingly) unrelated opportunities. Anytime you give a discount, think about giving it to your entire territory or customer base. Sales opportunities are not single isolated events. Here is why. Customers and prospects talk to each other. People switch companies. Companies buy other companies. It is not uncommon for one customer to find out he paid full price while everyone else got 40% off. What happens when that occurs? A good relationship can be spoiled very quickly and concessions may need to be made. The customer may lose faith in you and feel you've taken advantage of him. He may seek out your competition in the future. If he does choose to do business with you in the future, you can bet he is going to seek that 40%-off discount— and then some—to make up for the previous sales.

By leveraging the **7 Immutable Laws** *you create a consistent negotiation plan that coordinates negotiations across all your sales opportunities.*

7. Discounting allows your competitors to control your pricing and creates another hidden liability. Would you ever want to give your competitors the power to control your pricing and dictate your future success? Probably not. But when you discount to win business you do just that. Here is what a savvy competitor might do in a sales situation you are about to win—one in which they are about to lose. Imagine the following conversation between your competitor and the potential buyer—a buyer committed to selecting your company and wanting to do business with you.

Competitor: Ms. Buyer, I understand that we are not your first choice and you're going to go with the Winner Company. Is there anything we can do to prove our solution?

Buyer: No, we've made our decision to go with the Winner Company. I appreciate your asking, though.

Competitor: Are you absolutely sure?

Buyer: Yes, we're 100% certain.

Competitor: Is there anything at all we can do?

Buyer: No, there is nothing you can do. We are 100% sure we're going with the Winner Company.

Competitor: Ms. Buyer, I feel as though I have failed you in not proving our solution. It's my fault. Is there anything else I can do?

Buyer: No, there's nothing you can do. As I said, we're going to go with the Winner Company.

Competitor: I would sure hate for you to make the wrong decision because of something I did poorly.

Buyer: You did a good job. We just feel that the Winner Company is the best solution for us. Our decision is final and there is nothing you can do to change that. Our decision has been made.

Competitor: Ms. Buyer, I am sorry that I have failed you and failed to prove our solution. So please accept my apologies. However, if you are going to with the Winner Company, may I suggest that you speak to Mike Parker of the Harris Company? It is my understanding that he received an unbelievable discount from the Winner Company, one well in excess of 50%. You may want to compare notes. Would you like his number?

Buyer: Sure.

Competitor: Here is Mike's number: (212) 555-1212. His email is Mike.Parker@harriscompany.com.

Could one of your buyers be having this very conversation with a competitor right now? Would you want to give that power to your competitors? *When you discount to win business, you give pricing power to your competitors. By using the* **7 Immutable Laws** *you will keep your pricing power in your hands and out of your competitor's hands.*

8. Sales negotiation has a profound impact on the salesperson and sales team. Discounting means salespeople and sales teams earn less commission, and they have to work harder and work longer hours to make up the revenue shortfall. (See Figure 2)

When a salesperson discounts 10% he has to work an extra 11% harder to make up the short fall of revenue and reach his sales numbers. Based on a 40-hour work week, that is an extra 4 hours a week he will have to work. That means a half-day either Saturday or Sunday.

If the salesperson discounts 20%, he has to work an extra 25% harder to make up the revenue short fall. That is an extra 10 hours per week on top of his full-time job. That means an additional full day Saturday or

Discounting Impact Summary

Discount Level	% Work Harder	Extra Work Hours/Week (40-hour week)	Extra Work Hours/Week (50-hour week)	Lost Commission
10%	11%	4.4	5.6	?
20%	25%	10.1	12.5	?
30%	43%	17.1	21.4	?
40%	67%	26.7	33.3	?

Figure 2

Sunday and a couple of extra hours during the week.

When the salesperson discounts 30%, he has to work an extra 43% harder to make up the short fall of revenue and reach his sales numbers. That is an extra 17 hours per week—*over two extra days*. Forget having a weekend. He'll have to spend the entire weekend in the office—no fun at all.

Don't even ask about a 40% discount. A 40% discount rate means a salesperson has to work an additional 67% harder. That's 27 extra hours per week, or an extra 3 days (and then some) on top of his 40-hour-a-week job! This doesn't even begin to address the lost commission and wages the salesperson loses from discounting, and these numbers only get worse when you consider that the average salesperson already works about 50 hours per week.

Furthermore, how do you think these extra hours affect your salespeople? Does the extra work time create stress? Does it hinder quality family time? Does it adversely affect both mental and physical health? How about job satisfaction? Does it create turnover? Are "A" salespeople going to be attracted to this kind of environment? How will this affect your ability to attract and retain the best sales talent?

Not a pretty picture, is it?

9. A poor sales negotiation strategy initiates poor customer relationships — or prevents relationships from beginning at all. The inability to clearly execute a well-thought-out negotiation strategy adversely affects the buyer as well. After all, the purpose of a negotiation is to start a great relationship with the buyer. You want to expand and create even more value during the negotiation. You want to help him implement your solution so that he can increase his profits and market valuation. You want the buyer to clearly understand the value you are bringing to his organization. When you have a poor negotiation strategy and plan, negotiations can become contentious. Rather than expanding the pie and starting the relationship on a high note, both sides feel bloodied and evolve into a zero sum game or, worse yet, a negative sum game. Ill will can be created: Either the buyer or seller walks away from a sale that should be profitable for both parties, or the final agreement is delayed.

At best, a poor negotiation strategy leads to unprofitable deals for either one or both of the parties; often there is ultimately no agreement at all.

10. A well-defined sales negotiation strategy improves close rates and reduces the sales cycle by helping the salesperson to:

a. Know the end game. Most companies implement a negotiation strategy and plan in order to reduce discounting. As an added benefit they find that they increase their close rates and reduce their sales cycle as well. Why does this happen? First, when you implement a negotiation strategy and plan, your sales teams know what the endgame will look like; as a result they start selling better earlier in the sales cycle. They start to realize that negotiation takes place from the first sales call to the last, that it is not just something thrown together at the end. They learn to keep the conversation focused on the value created and spend little time defending price. They look for areas to expand the pie, making the relationship even better than the buyer expected, and they create value for both sides. Sales teams with a well-defined strategy make the buyer even more eager to do business with you. When it comes down to final negotiations, their well-thought-out plan is proactive in removing problems. They enable both parties to commit their resources to increase profitability and market valuation for their respective organizations.

Negotiation moves from a zero sum game to an act of creation, one that creates long-term partners.

b. Hit the window of opportunity while it's open. When sales negotiations become protracted the tone can become contentious and, worse yet, business priorities may shift and the allocated budget shift elsewhere. This then creates stalled opportunities that take longer to close and—even worse—opportunities that should close end up never closing at all because resources and priorities shift elsewhere. When this happens, the window of opportunity is missed for not only for the foreseeable future but, many times, forever.

Again, when you have a well-defined negotiation strategy and plan, your sales cycle shortens and your close rates accelerate.

When we work with companies, we find that their close rates increase from 5% to 30%. For example, if a company's close rate before implementing a negotiation strategy was 20% of deals in proposal, its new close rate after implementing the **7 Immutable Laws** will be from 25% to 50% of deals in proposal. This also creates a financial benefit to net income and market valuation. Using the company from Figure 1, if you improved your increased close rates by 5%, 10%, or 15% you would increase market valuation by 94%, 188%, and 282% respectively. When you look at the change in close rates coupled with the decrease in the discount rate, you see an even more profound increase in net income and market valuation. For example, if you increase close rates by 10% and reduce discounting by 10%, you will see a 298% increase in net income and market valuation, nearly *quadrupling* the company's present market valuation.

Ask yourself the following questions:

☑ Should having a sales negotiation plan and policy be part of my strategy?

☑ Is maintaining margin and price premiums important to me and my investors?

☑ Is there upside opportunity in my organization to increase revenues, net income, and market valuation?

☑ Does a discount on one sales opportunity affect other sales opportunities?

☑ Should I have a consistent negotiation policy and strategy?

☑ Is my current sales negotiation strategy creating hidden liabilities?

If you answered "yes" to any of the above questions, this book will be a great investment of your time.

Chapter 2
The Purpose
of Sales Negotiation

The purpose of negotiation is to start a great profitable long-term relationship for both parties, one that will increase the profitability and market valuation of both the buyer and the seller. We often hear the term "closing" used as if something is finished. Rather than finishing, however, you are really creating a new beginning. If this is a first-time sale, you are creating a new relationship. If you are extending an existing relationship, you are taking it to the next level. This relationship will help your buyer solve key business problems and allow the buyer to become more profitable and increase market valuation.

You are going to ask your buyer to make a commitment of resources. In return, you are going to commit your precious resources to this buyer. You both have to achieve the financial, business, and personal results that you are both after in order for your relationship to become a great long-term partnership. You both work together to enter into a longer-term relationship and co-create an agreement that will make your relationship better. If you use the **7 Immutable Laws** you can make that relationship better for you and the buyer—even more so than you or the buyer might have thought possible.

MORE ➤

Here are some of the key attributes we use to measure the success of a great sales negotiation. A great sales negotiation:

- starts a long-term profitable relationship for both parties;
- enables the seller to command a price premium;
- ensures the seller will get full asking price or more revenue than initially forecasted;
- ensures both the buyer and the seller grow the pie, each receiving more value at the end of the sales negotiation process than anticipated; and
- creates a buyer with a greater lifetime value.

Chapter 3
The Mindset of a Great Sales Negotiator and Closer

The act of negotiation is an act of collaboration and co-creation between you and the buyer. During the sales process, you have developed a relationship where you have demonstrated that you are uniquely and ideally suited to meet the needs of this buyer. You have demonstrated that you create unique value and you are the best solution for this buyer—more so than any of your competitors. By coming to a mutual agreement, you are both going to benefit. In fact, because you provide unique value you should command a price premium.

In the business world, resources, such as budget and people, are finite; priorities change and resources are reallocated all the time by both the buyer and seller. Your valuable resources are coveted and in demand by your existing clients and a pipeline of new prospects. The buyer's resources are in demand by many competing entities within his organization. You have both worked together and invested resources to look at how best to solve the buyer's problems. *The great salesperson and negotiator recognizes this situation and recognizes that now is the best time to dedicate these resources to solving the buyer's problem and creating a great long-term partnership.*

Rather than an adversarial approach, you are both going to work together to create, collaborate, and coauthor an agreement that is going to use this window of opportunity to make a great long-term partnership and commit each other's resources to each other in a profitable manner. *The best negotiators recognize that this is an opportunity to expand, create, and co-author an agreement that is even better than originally envisioned.* Using the **7 Immutable Laws** you should be able to get your full asking price, create more value for both you and the buyer, and take your relationship to the next level.

Key Items to Remember

• This is the start of a great profitable relationship for both parties.

• We are both going to commit valuable resources to each other.

• My mindset is: We will make this relationship better than either side could imagine separately.

Section II

The 7 Immutable Laws

Chapter 4
Immutable Law #1: You Must Be the Buyer's #1 Choice

Why Immutable Law #1 is important

You cannot discount your way to the #1 place. You must be the Buyer's #1 Choice before you begin to negotiate. If you are not the Buyer's #1 Choice, the buyer is using you and negotiating with you to beat down the real winner's price. If you *are* the number one choice, it is because you have put in a superior sales effort and proven that you are the best solution; therefore, you should command a price premium. *Never enter into a negotiation without knowing you are the Buyer's #1 Choice.*

Lower the Risk and Be the Clear #1 Choice.

I am often amazed by how many companies and salespeople start negotiating without knowing they are the clear winner. Their hopes are that they can discount their way to the #1 place. This is a terrible position to be in and a complete myth because, again, *you cannot discount your way to #1.* In business-to-business sales and sales of high-ticket products, people and companies do not buy price. They buy risk.

Risk comes in two forms: personal risks and business risks. Examples of personal risk are:

If we choose this vendor and the vendor relationship fails:

- Will I get fired?

- Will this sidetrack my 15-year career at the company where I put in tireless effort to move up the corporate ladder so I can one day be VP or CEO?

- Will I not get the bonus I need to add the extra room to my house, and leave my family very disappointed in me?

Examples of business risk are:

If we choose this vendor and the vendor's solution fails:

- Will it adversely affect our profits, shareholders, and employees?

- Will we lose good customers and prospects to the competition?

- Will we become uncompetitive in the marketplace?

If during your sales process you have put in a superlative effort and proven you are the least risky solution, you should command a price premium. Few, if any, buyers are going to worry about the marginal difference in price between solutions and vendors if they clearly believe you are going to deliver great economic benefits, and even fewer will risk their personal careers, lifestyle, take-home pay, and the hopes and dreams of their families to save some of the company's marginal dollars. It just doesn't happen that way.

The Simple Truth

The fact is, either you are the Buyer's #1 Choice or you aren't. Plain and simple. If you aren't the #1 Choice, don't negotiate. The buyer is using you to beat down the price of the real winner—your competitor. Your only solution is to go back and sell better. The only possible way you could discount your way to the #1 place is if all the competitors vying for the business have done an equally bad job of selling. In those rare instances, you may win low margin and unprofitable business as all the competitors slash prices and quickly race to the bottom. The better solution is to go back, sell better, and become the #1 Choice. Then you can command a price premium.

If you are already the #1 Choice, you have proven that you are the least risky solution. You have put in a superlative sales effort, distanced your-self from the competitor, and shown you create unique value. You there-fore should command a price premium and not discount to meet competitor's prices.

Always know you are the Buyer's #1 Choice before you enter into negotiation.

Elements of a Superlative Sales Effort

We have worked with numerous sales teams worldwide. Below are some of the elements we believe constitute a superlative sales effort, and while you don't have to have undertake/accomplish all of these elements, we highly recommend that you do. Negotiation success is the result of a superior sales effort. The weaker your sales effort, the geometrically worse your close rates become and the geometrically worse your dis-counting will become. In other words, accomplishing the following ele-ments during your sales process will ensure you are a lot better off in the final analysis:

- You have become the Buyer's #1 Choice (if not, you cannot begin to negotiate).

- You have a quantifiable payback/ROI cost justification agreed upon by the buyer and the seller.

- You know the business problems solved.

- You know the personal benefits of the solution for each decision maker.

- You know that each decision maker is a strong champion.

- You know the problems and price for the buyer if he takes no action.

- You have confirmed that the buyer knows your competitive advantages.

- You are proactive and know the budget and decision-making process.

- You know the ideal "go-live" date.

- You have proven you are the least risky solution.

- You know the buyer's compelling reason to move forward with the sale.

The more you have accomplished during your sales effort the better negotiator you will become. Negotiation success is a result of two things:

- You made a superlative sales effort, and

- You created and executed a strong negotiation plan.

Keep in mind that no amount of negotiation expertise can make up for a poor sales effort.

A superlative sales effort creates the potential to negotiate well. A strong negotiation plan will capitalize on that potential. A weak or non-existent negotiation plan will squander that potential.

Confirm You Are the Buyer's #1 Choice Before Entering into Negotiation.

Before you go into negotiation, you should know you are the #1 Choice in advance. You will then want to confirm that you are the *#1 Choice of the buyer*. During the course of a normal conversation, ask the buyer the following two questions:

- "All things being equal, would we be your first choice?"

- "Why?" or "Why not?"

If the buyer answers anything other than "yes" to the first question, find out what your shortcomings are and if they can be addressed, go back and sell better.

When the buyer answers "yes" to the first question and proceeds to answer the second question by telling you exactly why you are the best solution for him, this accomplishes two things:

- It confirms in the buyer's mind and in your mind the unique benefits that your solution delivers; and

- It provides the very reasons why you should command a premium for this sales opportunity.

Immutable Law #1 Action Items

Before you go into negotiation, ask yourself if you have accomplished the following:

- ☑ Have I put in a superlative sales effort?

- ☑ Have I confirmed that I am the Buyer's #1 Choice?

- ☑ If I am the **Buyer's #1 Choice**, it's time to start executing my negotiation plan.

- ☑ If I am NOT the **Buyer's #1 Choice,** I need to return to sell better.

Chapter 5
Immutable Law #2: You Must Know the Financial Benefit Your Solution Creates

---

Why Immutable Law #2 is important

If you don't know the financial benefit your solution provides, you will find yourself forced into a reactive negotiation position and you will be forced to defend your price rather than focus the negotiation on the value your solution provides. On the other hand, if you know the financial benefit you create, you also create a compelling reason to close and shorten the sales cycle.

Three types of negotiators

Knowing the financial benefit your solution provides is essential to being a good sales negotiator. I have found there are three types of salespeople:

Type 1: Salespeople who don't know the financial benefit of their solution. These salespeople are poor negotiators and closers. Why? They are constantly forced to defend their price. They are always on the defensive and their price and margins are quickly shredded to zero as they have no way of communicating or articulating concrete financial value; in order to create extra value they cut their price. We find this type of salesperson discounts on average from 30% to 65%.

Type 2: Salespeople who have done the financial analysis, but don't know how to use it effectively in negotiation. These salespeople typically give discounts of 15% to 40%. They are aware of the value that they are creating; however, they don't know how to leverage this information, focus the conversation on the financial benefits of their solutions, and maintain their margins.

Type 3: Salespeople who know the financial benefit their solution provides and use it effectively. These salespeople rarely give price discounts and are in a strong position to negotiate and close deals; they experience a higher close rate and shorter sales cycles because they know how to leverage this information and focus the conversation on the value delivered to the buyer. They leverage the financial information to create a sense of urgency and a compelling reason to close the sale. They also start a great relationship so the buyer can reap the financial benefit as soon as possible.

What type of financial analysis is best?

I've seen numerous types of financial analysis over the course of my career. Some are good, some are less good. My preferred method is to express the benefit as a yearly and monthly benefit to the buyer.

A less effective method is to use Return on Investment (ROI). While the ROI is a valuable number to know, the easiest way to increase the ROI of a solution is to reduce your price. While it does focus on the return your buyer can expect, it also concentrates the conversation on how to lower the investment as well. Which ultimately means lowering your price.

Another metric I try to steer clear of is Total Cost of Ownership (TCO), which says my solution costs less to use and implement than my competitors'. While this is a good number to know, TCO does not focus on value created. Instead it focuses the conversation on your costs and prices, not the unique value your solution creates.

Returning to my preferred method of expressing the benefit as a yearly and monthly benefit to the buyer, we look at *payback*, or the number of months it will take for your solution to pay for itself. So if, for example, your solution saves a company $500,000 a month and costs $2,000,000, the payback would be 4 months ($2,000,000 ÷ $500,000 savings a month = 4 months). Payback is an effective number to use, and though you can speed up the payback by reducing your asking price, in reality buyers will rarely expect—or ask—you to reduce your price when information is presented in this fashion.

A note about payback and strategic pricing

If you can show your solution has a payback of less than one year, you can usually get funds for your products and services from the buyer's operating budget rather than capital budget. Generally speaking, getting money from the operating budget requires fewer approvals, has shorter sales cycles, and is easier to close.

Know the monthly and annual benefit.

When using financial numbers in negotiation, I like to focus on annual and monthly benefit. This helps by focusing the conversation on the value you create, creating a sense of urgency, and creating a compelling reason to close the deal quickly. Suppose that, as in the above example, the annual benefit to the buyer is $6 million a year, which means the monthly benefit is $500,000. Here is how we might leverage this number in a discussion with the buyer.

Example:

Rep: From our analysis that we did together, our services will save your company $6 million a year. Is that correct?

Buyer: Yes.

Rep: Great. I would like to get your approval on the proposal so we can queue up our implementation team and speed this through our legal department. Then we can start saving your company as much money as quickly as possible. Each month of delay has a cost of $500,000. What are your thoughts?

Buyer: Not so fast; I think your price is too high.

Rep: When you say too high, what does that mean to you?

Buyer: I need at least a 20% discount.

Rep: So, about $400,000 off our $2,000,000 price?

Buyer: Yes.

Rep: I can certainly appreciate your request and as your rep and advocate I can forward your request and bring it to corporate. I don't know what their response to a request for a discount will be, and I don't know what, if any, discount they'll give you. I also don't know what new set of terms, conditions, and demands they'll want in return for a discount. I do know that any such request will take some time to review, and I do know this will put us at the back of line of the legal queue, and will therefore probably delay our ability to allocate resources and implement a solution for you for a minimum 4 to 6 months. Is it worth forgoing $2 million to $3 million in certain savings to try to get a $400,000 discount—if any at all is given? Please let me know your thoughts.

NOTE: In the above example, if I were selling lower cost solutions with a shorter sales cycle, I could change the annual benefit to monthly benefit and the monthly benefit to weekly benefit.

Keep it simple.

Keeping your financial analysis simple is crucial. I have seen some financial analysis that requires a Ph.D. in rocket science to understand. While that may be appropriate in some rare circumstances, keeping the analysis as simple as possible is usually better in most cases. Most financial decision makers do not want to pick their way through a detailed spreadsheet. Keeping it simple means creating a compelling business case that is easy to understand. I recommend having a spreadsheet of six to fifteen rows maximum. After that, your analysis becomes confusing to understand to anyone but the most technical of buyers. Bottom line it so the financial buyer can understand the financial implications your solution is going to have on his business.

Financial analysis must be agreed upon.

Both parties must co-author and agree upon the financial benefits. You may use a pre-existing spreadsheet to facilitate the analysis and discussion. Ideally, you should use that pre-existing spreadsheet to co-create the financial analysis with your prospect or client. Your buyer should actively participate in the creation of the analysis and agree on the results. The analysis does not have to be perfect to the penny. It does need to ballpark the financial benefit and give your buyer a clear understanding of the magnitude of this benefit.

What if your prospect doesn't agree with the analysis?

You and the buyer must agree on the analysis. Again, the analysis does not have to be perfect to the penny, but it does need to be in the ballpark to provide you and your buyer a clear understanding of the magnitude of the financial benefit. You and the buyer must also be in the same ballpark. A sale is a collaborative effort. Work with your buyer to understand his perspective. Use the buyer's numbers and assumptions to reach an agreement on the financial benefit. If your buyer is unable or unwilling to work with you, this may be a warning sign that this will not be a good relationship. When you and your buyer agree on the financial benefit, you are both able to focus on the long-term value, importance, and benefit of your relationship. *Agreeing on the financial analysis is the basis of good long-term partnership and is essential for a successful negotiation.*

Extend the pain chain.

If you can't communicate and define the value of your products and services you are destined to sell at very low margins. Every business must be able to quantify the value of its solutions. You can expand the value you create by examining the complete "pain chain". For example, a missed shipment of parts to a supplier can cause a rippling effect.

Production slows, utilization rates drop, and overtime might be required to pay workers to work longer when the parts arrive. Products may ultimately be shipped late. Shipping charges and express freight might be greater as a result. Customers may call in because the products they need to run their businesses are delayed. Support calls and support costs jump. Your clients may seek other vendors. You may lose some clients completely. Others might reduce the amount of business they do with you. If you are the supplier who offers "100% on-time delivery," quantify what that really means to your buyer by examining the complete pain chain.

Advanced technique

If you want to make the value you create even larger, tie the value of your offering to the increase in market valuation of your buyer's business. While there are many ways to measure the market value of a company (generally speaking, market value is the amount a buyer would pay to purchase the company), most companies are valued as a multiple of the amount of income they generate. If your solution will save a company $5 million a year—that's great. Public companies are typically valued at a multiple of net income, also called "earnings". That multiple is called the price/earnings ratio. If you save a company $5 million a year, that is $5 million more gross profit the company will enjoy. If there were no taxes, that would drop $5 million to the bottom line (earnings). If the company's price/earnings ratio was 20 (meaning the value of the company was 20 x its earnings), the market value of the firm would increase by $100 million ($5 million in earnings x 20 price/earnings ratio). The marginal price premium for your offering would be miniscule compared to the $100 million in market valuation you are creating. Those numbers create a compelling reason to close!

Here is how you can factor in for taxes. In the above example, suppose the company had a 35% tax rate, of the $5 million in profits 35% would be taken out for taxes. In this case, the buyer would have to pay $1.75

million in taxes ($5 million x 35% tax rate). That would leave $3.25 million in earnings ($5 million − $1.75 million in taxes). With a price/earnings ratio of 20, you would increase the buyer's market valuation by $65 million ($3.25 million x 20). Indeed, a very compelling financial reason to close.

Private companies are typically valued as a multiple of their "Earnings Before Interest Taxes and Depreciation and Amortization" or EBITDA. The general range on market valuation for private companies is 6 to 12 times EBITDA. So if your buyer were a private company and your solution saved your buyer $5 million a year, it would increase the company's market valuation from $30 million to $60 million ($5 million x 6 = $30 million, $5 million x 12 = $60 million). Again, a very compelling reason to close the sale for the buyer.

NOTE: EBITDA is a "before tax" number so you do not have to worry about factoring in taxes.

This analysis may seem a bit difficult, but it is not as complicated as it may first appear. If it is confusing, contact your CFO or an accountant. Once you get the hang of it, the time and money you spend in learning this analysis will be well rewarded.

Losing 60% to 80% negotiating power

As I've mentioned, we run our negotiation training and consulting programs worldwide across many industries. When we ask our participants how much negotiating power they lose when they don't know the final value their products create, the typical answer is between 60% to 80%. While this is not scientific, it does show the extreme importance of knowing the financial benefit you create and why **Immutable Law #2** is essential.

MORE ➤

Immutable Law #2 Action Items

Before you go into negotiation, ask yourself if you have accomplished the following:

☑ Do I know the financial value my solution provides to my buyer?

☑ Have I co-authored and agreed upon the benefit with the buyer?

☑ Do I know the monthly benefit?

☑ Do I know the annual benefit?

☑ Bonus points if I can relate those benefits to the change in market valuation.

Chapter 6
Immutable Law #3: Anticipate Getting Squeezed On Price

 Anticipate getting squeezed on price. Withstand squeezes by focusing in on value and giving a firm and polite "No."

Why Immutable Law # 3 is important

Price negotiation is *not* cost justification. If you are the Buyer's #1 Choice, your buyer wants to buy from you. The next question is, "What is the lowest price I can get it for?" Buyers will try to squeeze you on price. You must be prepared to resist squeezes by refocusing the conversation on the benefits of your solution. *By refocusing on the benefits of the solution, you are giving a polite "no" to their request for a discount and offering them a face-saving way to agree to the sale.*

It's just business.

Price negotiation is *not* cost justification. It is the buyer's financial responsibility to try to get your product and services for the lowest price possible. It is not his fault, and it is not personal; it is just his job. Your job is to get your maximum asking price. Buyers will squeeze you at least once; savvy buyers will squeeze you multiple times. A squeeze is simply nothing more than request for a discount. By refocusing on the benefits of your solution, giving your buyer a polite "no" to his request (for which you are under no obligation), and providing a face-saving way to agree, you can both move forward. In fact, not only are you under no obligation to provide a discount, you should be commanding a price premium. In business-to-business complex sales and sales of high-value items, people and companies buy risk. If during your sales process you have proven that you are uniquely and ideally suited to solve their problems and you have shown that you are the least risky solution, you are entitled to command a price premium.

How does the buyer know he has gotten the best price from you?

Buyers know they have gotten the best price from you when you refuse to give in. Think of this simple analogy. If you had a completely dry towel, how many times do you think someone would squeeze that towel in order to squeeze some water out of it? One, maybe two, or three squeezes maximum before the person gave up and realized there was no water to be gotten. But how many times would that person squeeze a wet towel? Many times, wouldn't he? The person would keep squeezing and squeezing as long as water continued to come out. When the water stops flowing, he may continue wringing to get every last drop. Even when he's gotten every last drop out, he may try squeezing the towel a couple more times to make sure he's gotten everything.

It's a slippery slope.

The same is true of your negotiation. The more firm you are about resisting squeezes the more quickly buyers will stop squeezing. Once you start giving, they will continue squeezing. The more you give the more and harder they will squeeze. Once you give a little, you have given the signal that there are discounts and extra items to be had. You have positively rewarded their squeezes with a discount. This only invites more price squeezes. It's an unhappy cycle. The more you appease, the more they will squeeze. Your job is to anticipate getting squeezed and stop the squeezes early on. You must be the dry towel!

Be prepared for being squeezed on price.

Anticipate getting squeezed on price, know it is coming, and look forward to it. Know that buyers will try multiple times. Recognize the situation and be proactive and prepared for the squeezes. Simply give the polite "no" by refocusing the conversation on the benefits and value of your solution. Be proactive and prepared to withstand squeezes in advance with well-thought-out responses that focus the conversation on the benefits to the buyer. I usually like to have no fewer than 7 responses prepared in advance of every negotiation. In fact, you might become disappointed if the buyer doesn't try to squeeze you.

Here are approaches you may want to take to defend yourself from squeezes and refocus the conversation back on value delivered and how the buyer wins. Remind the buyer of:

- business problems solved
- personal problems solved
- the problems and price of taking no action
- the positive impact of a solution
- your unique competitive advantages
- the current inefficient process
- the ideal go-live date

Squeeze 1

Rep: I would love to get your approval on the proposal so we can queue up our implementation team. What are your thoughts about moving forward?

Buyer: I think your price to too high; you're going to have to sharpen your pencil.

Rep: When you say too high, what does that mean to you?

Buyer: I need at least a 15% discount.

Rep: Mr. Buyer, I thought we agreed that this proposal was going to help solve your inventory problem.

Buyer: Yes, it will.

Rep: And your business will run much better because of it?

Buyer: Yes, it will.

Rep: Great. Then since this is the price to do the job correctly and deliver the best solutions to your problems, I would enjoy getting your agreement and commitment so we can commit our resources to you.

Squeeze 2

Buyer: Not so fast. I still I need some discount.

Rep: When you say that you need some discount, can you tell me more about that?

Buyer: I just need it.

Rep: You mentioned that last week your inventory problem caused you to miss shipment and caused customers to call and cancel orders. Is that correct?

Buyer: Yes, it did.

Rep: How quickly would you like to solve this problem?

Buyer: Immediately.

Rep: Great, this price will get you into our queue so we can solve this problem quickly. I want to get you into the queue as soon as possible so we can hit your implementation deadline. What are your thoughts about moving forward?

Squeeze 3

Buyer: I still need to get some discount.

Rep: We crafted this proposal and right-sized it for your business.

If we reduce our price by 15% we would have to take out significant parts of the proposal. Is there anything you would like to see taken out of the proposal?

Buyer: No, not at all. I like the proposal.

Squeeze 4

Buyer: I just need a lower price.

Rep: You mentioned that you needed to have the solution implemented by January 15th. Is that still correct?

Buyer: Yes.

Rep: What would happen if we missed that date or the solution was not correctly implemented?

Buyer: A lot of bad things...I don't even want to think about it.

Rep: How important is it that this solution is implemented by January 15th—and done correctly the first time?

Buyer: It's essential.

Rep: This is the proposal that will properly enable us to accomplish that goal and hit your January 15th timeline. What are your thoughts about moving forward?

Buyer: If we come to an agreement, are you sure we will be successfully up and running by January 15th?

Rep: If you can get us a signed agreement by the close of business, we sure can.

Buyer: Are you sure?

Rep: Yes, absolutely. And won't it be great when we get this problem fixed?

Buyer: Okay, let's do it.

NOTE: You will develop your own style and ways of handling squeezes. Always be positive and upbeat. You are going to create a profitable business relationship between both organizations, one in which you and the buyer prosper. You are there to facilitate the start of a great relationship. You are only going to enhance your credibility by sticking to your values and price. When you discount, in essence you are telling the buyer *my price is not the real price and I gave you a fake price, one I thought you would be foolish enough to accept*. That runs completely counter to the great long-term relationship you want to establish. In fact, it erodes your credibility. Is that anyway to start or expand a relationship? Of course not.

Immutable Law #3 Action Items

Before you go into negotiation, ask yourself if you have accomplished the following:

- ☑ Am I prepared to recognize and identify squeezes?
- ☑ Have I prepared a list of 7 ways to respond to squeezes by giving a firm and polite "no" and by refocusing the conversation on the benefits of my solution?
- ☑ Am I prepared to be the dry towel?

Chapter 7

Immutable Law #4: Be Proactive on Budget and Remove Decision-Making Obstacles in Advance

Be proactive by knowing the budget and decision-making process before you enter into negotiation. Have budget allocated in advance of your negotiation and remove obstacles before you encounter them.

Why Immutable Law # 4 is important

If you don't know the budget and decision-making process, you are likely to have to cut price to fit in "this year's budget" and/or get beat up along the path completing the sale. If you know the budget and decision-making process, you can proactively remove obstacles that you may encounter and proactively get budget allocated from the current budget and future budgets so that you can command price premiums and get your full asking price—or better.

Just the facts

In any sales opportunity, you will want to know five key pieces of information before you go into negotiation:

- What is their current budget?
- Who controls the budget and how are decisions made?
- Where else can budget come from?
- When is the next budgeting cycle?
- What obstacles can get in the way?

It surprises me that some salespeople and sales organizations go into negotiation without knowing this information in advance. Then they are shocked to learn that their buyer or customer doesn't have enough budget for their product or services—even though you both have been through a detailed sales cycle where you have spent resources learning about your buyer's needs, developed a great relationship, and proved that your product is uniquely and ideally suited for the buyer's company. Salespeople come to the end of a sales cycle not clearly knowing if there is budget for their full suite of services, and are unclear about the decision-making process needed to get their full asking price. It is critical that you know this information early on in the sales cycle.

Be proactive and have budget allocated in advance of negotiation.

Always know when your prospect goes into his next budgeting cycle. If you are in a long, complex sales cycle, your sales cycle may take three months, six months, or a year; you will either cross or be likely to come upon another budgeting horizon. This gives you the opportunity to allocate money from multiple years' budgets: this year's, next year's and future years'. Be proactive. If there is not enough budget in this year's plan, get the buyer to allocate ample budget, and then some, from next year's budget. This will eliminate the **Not In Our Budget Syndrome**, or **NIBS**. This familiar cry can be heard in just about every negotiation, and is used as a squeeze. *Be proactive and prepared: During your sales cycle, make sure your buyer has budget allocated in advance of your negotiation.*

Remove obstacles to getting your full asking price before you encounter them.

You will want to be proactive in your understanding of the decision-making and buying process. If final purchases and prices are negotiated by the purchasing department, coach your prospect up front, and let the buyer know in advance that your terms and prices are the real terms and that these are prices you do not discount. If you are speaking to the financial buyer (the buyer whose budget will be used, whose career will benefit from the implementation of your products and services, and who has his skin in the game when your solution is chosen and implemented), let him know in advance that if his final decision is being made by the purchasing department and will be determined by the lowest price bidder, then this opportunity is not appropriate for your company. You can then politely walk away from the sales opportunity.

If the buyer is looking for the best solution rather than the lowest priced solution then this could be a great sales opportunity. Be proactive:

- Coach the buyer early in the sales process that you will need his personal support to push the full price through the purchasing department.

- Prepare the buyer. Let the buyer know that if the purchasing department tries to squeeze you for a lower price, none is possible.

- Align your goals with the buyer's goals. Let him know that squeezes and a protracted negotiation from the purchasing department may delay the implementation of the solution, and may cause him to take on additional costs and risks as your resources to complete, implement, or finalize the sale may be reallocated during a lengthy negotiation with the purchasing team. You and your buyer are a team. Together, you are competing for your company's resources. These same resources are being sought after by your current customer base, and other salespeople with a whole pipeline of new prospects. Your buyer's resources are also being sought after by other entities within his organization.

You and your buyer both win when you get the past the obstacles in the purchasing department. One word from the financial buyer is all it usually takes to push a deal through purchasing. Though many companies will tell you the final decision is being made by the purchasing department, rarely, if ever, is this the case for a sale that involves a significant degree of risk. (By the way, the financial buyer typically uses the purchasing department as the bad guy to get your products and services for the lowest price possible. It's just another squeeze.) *So be proactive, know the decision-making process, and remove obstacles before you encounter them.*

What to do if you are in a reactive negotiating position

After reading this book you should never, ever, find yourself in a reactive negotiating position again. However, if you are currently negotiating a sales opportunity and you are in a reactive mode, please follow this 4-step process.

- Ask your prospect about his current budget.
- Take the difference between his budget and your full asking price and make it as small as possible.
- Ask your prospect where else he can get additional budget.
- Ask your prospect when he will be able to get additional budget.

Example:

Rep: Our total package is $100,000.

Buyer: That's not in our budget.

Rep: How much is in the current budget?

Buyer: We only have $70,000.

Rep: We're only $30,000 apart. Over the next three years of use that's only $10,000 per year. Put another way, for the 100 users of our services, that's only $100 per year, per user. There are 250 working days per year. That turns out to be $0.40 a day per user to make your most vital resources—your employees—more efficient. In fact, if this project is successful we will improve employee productivity by 15%, increase net income by $3 million per year, and increase your market valuation by $60 million. Where can we find budget for $0.40 per day per employee so you can reap those great financial rewards?

Buyer: I guess I can get an extra $15,000 from Tom's budget.

Rep: Great, where else can we get the other $0.20 cents a day?

Buyer: I'm not sure.

Rep: Please tell me about the time frame for the next budgeting cycle.

Buyer: New budgets are set in two months.

Rep: Great, by the time the contract goes through legal and you get invoiced, it will be two months. Can we allocate money from that fresh budget?

Buyer: I guess I can make some adjustments.

Rep: What are your thoughts about making those adjustments?

Buyer: It's doable.

Rep: If you can commit to an agreement and shepherd the paper work through legal, I can commit to getting you into our priority implementation queue. That way we can allocate resources, make sure we implement the solution, and have your team trained by the June 30th window, which is the critical date to launch this project. What are your thoughts?

Buyer: Okay, let's do it.

MORE ➤

The optimal time to have this conversation

While the above example is simplified, this is exactly the conversation you will want to have with the financial buyer early on in the sales cycle before negotiation—not during the final stages of negotiation. The ability to understand the benefits your prospect or client is gaining, to understand the budget and decision-making process, and to proactively manage current budgets and future budgets is critical to maintaining your margins and getting full asking price.

Immutable Law #4 Action Items

Before you go into negotiation, ask yourself if you have accomplished the following:

- ☑ Do I know the buyer's current budget?
- ☑ Do I know who controls the budget and how decisions are made?
- ☑ Do I know where more budget can come from?
- ☑ Do I know when the next budgeting cycle is?
- ☑ Have I proactively gotten budget allocated for this year and future years' budgets?
- ☑ Have I proactively addressed and managed any obstacles that may come up with purchasing and in the decision-making process?

Chapter 8

Immutable Law #5:
Expand the Pie with a Set
of Non-Monetary Trade-Ups

Expand the pie and create more value with a set of non-monetary trade-ups that deliver more value to your buyer and more value to you.

Why Immutable Law # 5 is important

You have the opportunity to increase the value you deliver to your buyer and at the same time create more value for yourself as well. You can do this while still maintaining a price premium by creating a set of non-monetary trade-ups.

Creating more value for your buyer

You have the opportunity to increase the value delivered to your client with items that have little or no cost to you and deliver great value to your buyer. For example, if the product or service you sell requires training, you might expand the pie by offering "to have 5 extra people attend training at no cost." The value of that training might be worth $2,000 per person. So you have created value and expanded the pie by $10,000 (5 people x $2,000 per person). The cost of those 5 extra people at training might be a few sandwiches and some extra manuals—the cost would even be less if you were doing Web-based training—in other words, practically zero. The value to your buyer is $10,000 and greater. The buyer will now have 5 extra people trained who know how to use your products and services, and your client will now likely derive more benefit and value from your offering by having more people correctly trained to utilize your solution. Additionally, you have added more value and helped lower the risk of the purchase. In business-to-business complex sales and sales of high-dollar products and services, the buyer chooses the best vendor based on *risk*, not price. Now the buyer will not have to worry about what happens when trained people leave the organization as there will be 5 extra people capable of instantly filling those roles. You will have created great value to the buyer.

Some "gives" you may want to consider include:

- extending payment terms
- placing in priority implementation queue
- providing extra training
- providing on-site training
- provisioning extra users
- providing extra licenses
- loaning add-on tools or modules
- offering priority support
- leads or introductions
- creating a press release or other marketing assets
- having key personnel or uniquely qualified personnel assigned to work with the buyer

Never give without getting.

Never give without getting is a fundamental of negotiation and sales. When you offer to give something you should get something in return. Therefore, you will want to create a list of "gets" — things that you want in return. So if, for example, you are giving "5 extra people sales training", what do you want to get in return?

Some "gets" you may want are:

- payment upfront or accelerated payment terms
- longer-term commitment

- more users
- guarantee of future business
- case studies
- metrics
- to serve as a reference or speak at a conference
- referrals to other parts of the organization
- referrals to third parties
- press releases
- maintenance paid in advance

These are just some suggested "gets". Please feel free to customize and tailor these "gets" to create your own list.

Hidden benefits

Some "gives" not only benefit the buyer, but can benefit the seller as well. If you are giving "5 extra people training", won't that benefit the seller as well? If more people are trained on your product, won't that increase the value of your offering? Will it help your company's products and services become part of the buyer's corporate fabric? When it comes time to renew or replace your products, will you be in a stronger position to get the repeat business and insulate yourself from competitors? If your buyer needs ancillary products or add ons, is he more likely to buy from you? Absolutely—to all of the above. And if a trained user leaves the buyer's organization is he likely to recommend your products and services to new a new employer? Definitely. "Extra people at training" is a great "give" for many businesses. It is a give that also serves as a "get" as well—after all, the buyer is investing additional resources in learning your product.

Ranking "gives"

To expand the pie for both parties, create a list of potential "gives". Identify those "gives" that have high value to your buyer. Next look at the list and identify those that have low cost to you. You can now see which ones add great value to your clients with minimal or no cost to you. These now become great "gives" to offer in return for "gets" to grow the pie and increase the value of the deal for your buyer. Also, make note of "gives" that create hidden value for you—as in the example above. If a "give" adds high value to the buyer, is low or zero cost to you, and creates hidden value for you, this is a "give" you will definitely want to offer as a first choice.

Ranking "gets"

This is just like the exercise above to expand the pie—creating a list of potential "gets". Identify those "gets" that have high value to you. Next, look at the list and identify those that have low cost to your buyer. You can now see which ones add great value to you with minimal cost to your buyer. These now become great "gets" to ask for in return for "gives".

Creating a list of trade-ups that will expand the pie

Based on your ranking you can create a list of "gives" and "gets" that will grow the pie and expand the value of the relationship with your buyer to new heights.

Here is an example of a trade-up chain from one of our clients, a software company:

Non-Monetary Trade-Ups

"GIVES"	"GETS"
• Extra people at training	• Extra years on contract
• Priority implementation	• Payment upfront • Maintenance paid in advance
• 60-day payment terms	• Metrics • Case study • Press release

Note that all the "gives" above have very little extra cost and can deliver great value to the buyer.

Over time you can create a standard trade-up chain that becomes a corporate standard and that will enable reps to consistently satisfy buyers, win deals, and reduce the sales cycle. It also reduces the amount of management time needed to close sales opportunities. You can also bundle together the "gives" and "gets". In other words, you may offer one "give" for multiple "gets". For example, you may offer to give "5 additional people training" if your buyer will commit to 2 extra years on the contract and serve as a reference for 5 future prospects.

NOTE: You don't have to wait till the end of the sales cycle to expand the pie. You can start proposing these trade–ups earlier on in the sales cycle to help distance yourself from the competition.

Immutable Law #5 Action Items

Before you go into negotiation, ask yourself if you have accomplished the following:

☑ Have I created a list of non-monetary "gives" that:

- Identifies those "gives" that are high value to the buyer and low cost to me?

- Identifies those "gives" that actually create value to me as well?

☑ Have I created a list of "gets" that:

- Identifies those "gets" that are high value to me and low cost to the buyer?

- Identifies those "gets" that actually create value to the buyer?

☑ Based on the two lists, have I created a set of non-monetary trade-ups that will expand the pie?

☑ Over time, am I looking to develop a standardized set or bundles of trade-ups?

Chapter 9
Immutable Law #6:
Never Give Without Getting

Never give without getting; if you must give a price discount to the buyer, make sure you get something of equal or greater value in return.

Why Immutable Law #6 is important

"Never give without getting" is a fundamental of negotiation. If you give without getting the buyer will perceive that "give" to have little value and it will have set you up for future discounting with the buyer on future sales opportunities—as well as encourage him to ask for more discounts on this sale.

Make sure you get something of high value in return.

If you have to give a price discount, and we rarely suggest you do, make sure you get something of high value in return. When you reduce your price you geometrically reduce your profitability. It is the most costly "give" you can make. Make sure you get something in return of equal— or preferably greater—value. You want to create a set of monetary trade-offs. The deeper the discount you offer the buyer, the more you must ask in return. If you do not ask for anything in return, the buyer will have little respect for your "give", which only encourages him to ask for more.

Never give without getting.

As we discussed in **Immutable Law #5,** *never give without getting* is a fundamental of negotiation. In **Immutable Law #5,** we discussed non-monetary "gives" — "gives" where the value to the buyer is greater than the cost to the seller. For example, "giving extra people at training" had a value of $10,000 and only cost you maybe $200 to $300. In return, you got valuable "gets". In **Immutable Law #6**, however, we are talking specifically about financial "gives" — i.e., discounts. Discounts are the costliest "gives" a buyer can ask for. A $10,000 discount costs you $10,000. That's why it is almost always preferable to use non-monetary "gives" from **Immutable Law #5,** *before* giving any discounts. In fact, do not consider giving a discount until you have completely exhausted all the options available with **Immutable Law #5**. By doing so you will be able to reduce or entirely eliminate discounting. (More about this topic later in the chapter.)

Create a list of "gets" that are ideal for you.

Identify "gets" that you want in return from your buyer. Some things you may want to "get" are:

- payment upfront or accelerated payment terms
- longer term commitment
- more users
- guarantee of future business
- case studies
- metrics
- to serve as a reference or speak at a conference
- referrals to other parts of the organization
- referrals to third parties
- press release
- maintenance paid in advance

These are just some common "gets"; please feel free to customize and create your own list of "gets" that are perfect for your business.

Rank your gets.

You will want to rank your "gets". Define the "gets" that are high value to you. Then look at your list of "gets" and identify the ones that are low cost to your buyer. "Gets" that are high value to you and low cost to your buyer should be easily attainable and can be part of most negotiated agreements.

Create a monetary trade-off chain.

You can now create a monetary trade-off chain. The more the buyer demands from you the more you must demand from the buyer. You have proven you are the #1 Choice to the buyer and that you create unique value. You should command a price premium. If you are giving a price discount you will want to get items of equal or greater value. You should expect to get the "gets" that are high value to you and low cost to your buyer. You should not be afraid to ask for "gets" that are high value to you and costly to your buyer. If they are asking you for costly "gives", you can ask for costly "gets". You can also if you wish ask for a bundle of "gets". Make sure you include items that are high value to you and low cost to your buyer in your bundle.

Here is an example of a trade-off chain you might create:

Monetary Trade-Offs	
"GIVES"	**"GETS"**
5% discount	• Extra 2 years on contract • Case study • Serve as reference to 5 prospects
10% discount	• Extra 3 years on contract • Payment upfront • Case study • Serve as reference to 5 prospects
15% discount	• Extra 4 years on contract • Payment upfront • Case study • Serve as reference to 10 prospects

Just as with **Immutable Law #5**, over time you can create a standard trade-off chain that becomes a corporate standard. This will enable reps to consistently satisfy buyers, win deals, and reduce the sales cycle. It will also reduce the amount of sales management time need to close sales opportunities.

Best practices on discounting

If you do give a discount, and again we suggest you rarely do, make sure you note it as a one-time special discount amount. In your contract and proposal, clearly mark the "gets" you are receiving and present the discount as an absolute dollar discount and not as a percent discount. Why, you may ask? When your proposals include a 20% discount—or any percentage—this will become the *legacy discount percentage* that the buyer will expect in future sales situations. You are creating both a future expectation and a corporate liability. You are also reducing the lifetime value of your buyer. By putting the absolute dollar amount together with the "gets" you receive, the buyer is prevented from establishing a discounting legacy or creating an ongoing discounting expectation. This increases the lifetime value of your client and makes future sales at full asking price easier.

Avoid a common mistake: Never give a "wink-wink" price.

I have seen this happen many times in my career and I want to make sure you don't make this common mistake. Salespeople often submit pricing proposals or give pricing amounts by saying, "This is the price, but we can do better if you're serious," or "We can sharpen our pencil, if we have to." I call this the "wink-wink price". *Never give a wink-wink price.* What this tells the buyer is that your price is not the real price. The first discount you give will be the price from which they start negotiating. The value of your first discount will be perceived as worthless and you will get nothing in return. You will have just violated **Immutable Law #6.** In other words, you will have given without getting anything in return. If your price is high and shocks your buyer—great. If you finally do give a discount the buyer will understand and perceive the value of that discount and you will get something in return for that "give". When you communicate to the buyer that your first price is not the real price you have undermined your credibility—and that is not a good thing.

NOTE: This "Never Give Without Getting" **Immutable Law**, like all the others, should be applied during your complete sales cycle. So, for example, if your buyer wants you to "give" him a demonstration of your product, decide what commitments and "gets" you want in return. You may ask for or require an hour discovery call with the CFO before the meeting or require some other "get".

"Can you meet me half way?" A very profitable question

If you are giving a discount and the buyer is agreeable to your trade-offs, ask one last question: "Can you meet me half way?" You may be surprised at the number of times the answer will be yes, or the buyer will counter with an offer of a lower discount. Asking this simple question is a great way to reduce your discounting and geometrically increase your profits, if you do discount.

Is discounting necessary?

The last time you gave a discount, what was magical about that number? Whether you gave 5%, 10%, 20%, or 40%, what magically happened? Did you suddenly hit a financial hurdle rate on the sale that suddenly made the sale a go for the buyer? Unlikely. And if you did, you should probably walk away from the sale as the upside for the buyer is small and if anything goes wrong (as it invariably will), you are going to have a very unhappy customer. What was magical about 5%? Why wasn't it 4% or 6%? What was magical about 10%? Why wasn't it 9% or 11%? What was magical about 20%? Why wasn't it 19% or 21%? You get the picture. The number was probably arbitrary. So what does that really mean to you? You probably unnecessarily gave away money and profits.

Could you have used Immutable Law # 5 to make a better deal and grow the pie?

If on a $100,000 sales opportunity you discounted 10% and gave away a $10,000 discount to the buyer, couldn't you have offered $10,000 worth of extra training that only cost you a few sandwiches and some manuals? What about $20,000 worth of extra training…or even $30,000 worth of extra training that only costs you a few hundred dollars? Wouldn't that be a better agreement for the buyer? In addition, would the buyer likely derive more value from implementing your solution? Wouldn't you have also lowered the buyer's risk? Would that have been a better agreement for you? Trading off dollars rarely accomplishes much and adds little to the value of the sale. It certainly doesn't lower the buyer's risk. If the solution fails, no one is going to care about the few marginal dollars saved. Are there non-monetary "gives" that can lower the buyer's risk and increase the value of your solution? Always ask yourself what other non-monetary items you can substitute instead of giving money in return for my "gets".

Discounting is BS.

Why is it that some reps selling the same products to the same types of clients will have a 0% discount rate, while others will have a 40% discount rate? It is because discounting is BS. No, not "Bull S—". "Belief System." Reps who sell value and know they are the #1 Choice of the buyer believe they don't have to discount to win opportunities and hence they don't. Others believe they have to discount to win sales opportunities and hence they do. If you are the #1 Choice, you have earned the right to command a price premium. Therefore, remember these important facts:

- You cannot discount your way to #1.
- Price negotiation is not cost justification.
- People buy risk, not price.

Further evidence that discounting is BS.

Have you ever worked for a company that had some issues which were not negotiable and would not make any concessions on those issues no matter what? For example, maybe the company would never, under any circumstances, make certain modifications to its product. Or perhaps the company always insisted on partial payment upfront. Why are these issues non-negotiable? How did they become untouchable? The answer is simple. The company simply decided to make them non-negotiable. How did the company do that? It tells the buyer the issues are non-negotiable from the start and sticks to that belief. Do you currently have some issues that you will not concede, no matter what? How do you do that? Why can't your price be one of them?

Quick Summary

If you use **Immutable Laws #1** through **#5**, you will rarely have to discount. In fact, you may completely eliminate discounting altogether. Not only that, you will also increase your win rates and create better agreements for both parties. Change your belief system. *If you do offer monetary discounts, make sure you get something of equal or greater value in return!*

Immutable Law #6 Action Items

Before you go into negotiation, ask yourself if you have accomplished the following:

☑ Have I created a monetary trade-off chain of "gives" and "gets"?

☑ Have I reviewed my monetary trade-off chain, and investigated where I can substitute non-monetary "gives" for discounts?

☑ Have I gone back and reviewed **Immutable Laws #1** through **#5** before I give any discount?

☑ Have I changed my belief system on discounting and watched the positive results?

Chapter 10
Immutable Law #7:
Know Your Walk-Away Price and Conditions

Why Immutable Law # 7 is important

When you are prepared to walk away, the buyer knows he has gotten all he can out of you. It also allows the buyer to rethink his position and consider the poor alternatives, which may occur by not completing a sale with you.

It's not enjoyable, but it's necessary.

You must know your walk-away price. This signals to buyers that you cannot give anymore and that they have gotten all they can out of you. If you have qualified the opportunity correctly and used **Immutable Laws #1** through **#5**, and you have exhausted the trade-off chain from **Immutable Law #6**, you should rarely, if ever, find yourself in this position.

As a professional, you know this is business, it is not personal. If you have used **Immutable Laws #1** through **#6** correctly, you have done the best you can. You have negotiated in good faith and so has your buyer. The buyer simply wanted terms and conditions that you cannot make. He will be forgoing the huge financial value you created from **Immutable Law #2** (knowing the financial benefit your solution creates). You have proven that you are uniquely qualified to help his business. You have used a superlative sales effort to clearly position yourself as the #1 Choice (**Immutable Law #1**) and proven you are the lowest risk solution. You will be forgoing marginally profitable business. It is a lose-lose situation. But even then it's important to take a closer look at who has more at stake.

Resetting the playing field

Though it is a lose-lose situation, it does reset the playing field. Generally speaking, the buyer will be losing a lot more than you are. He will not be getting the financial benefit of your solution. His alternatives are to move forward with an inferior supplier or not complete the purchase at all—in other words, suffer the problems and pay the price of inaction. He will be stuck with having the very same problems that led the company to seek a solution in the first place. You will have lost marginally profitable business at best. Your upside is that you will have freed your resources to win much more profitable business and you have potentially avoided unprofitable business. So, under this scenario, who has more to lose? That's right, the buyer.

When you walk away, you give the buyer time to rethink and reassess his position, and this is usually to your benefit.

How to walk away

Always walk away politely. The same people you are walking away from are the same people you may be doing business with either in the long term or short term, whether at their present company or another. So be prepared to walk away politely. You will also want to get their best offer and ask the following questions:

- What price and conditions are you seeking?

- At that price and those conditions, what can I say to our management team that you are willing to offer in return?

MORE ➤

Your options once you walk away

Once you have gotten the buyer's best offer you have three options:

- You can politely walk away from the business.
- You can come back with a counter offer.
- You can accept the buyer's price and terms.

1. **Politely walking away from this buyer's business.** Be kind and let him know that you cannot commit your company's resources under those terms and conditions, and wish him the best of luck. You may be surprised at his reaction. He may reassess his position and come to you with an alternative.

2. **Coming back to the buyer with a counter offer.** After reassessing his alternatives, including the personal risk involved in selecting the wrong vendor, he may be much more agreeable to a counter offer.

3. **Agreeing to the buyer's terms and conditions.** I generally would not recommend this strategy as it sets a bad precedent for a relationship with the buyer, and creates a legacy of discounting and treating you as a commodity provider. As we discussed earlier, a discount on one sale is not an isolated event. It can—and usually does—have a rippling effect across current and future buyers and can ultimately create a corporate liability.

Conclusion on walking away

If you use **Immutable Laws #1** through **#6**, you should rarely if ever be in this situation. In sales it is tough to walk away; however, it is a very necessary strategy. When you are the number #1 Choice of the buyer and you walk away, you force the buyer to consider his alternatives. This will usually put you in a stronger position. Some clients are not worth having; walking away from a sale can mean thanking yourself for heading off future trouble with this buyer.

Immutable Law #7 Action Items

Before you go into negotiation, ask yourself if you have accomplished the following:

- ☑ Do I know my walk-away price and conditions before I enter into negotiation?

- ☑ Do I know how to politely walk away?

- ☑ Do I remember that walking away will strengthen my position?

- ☑ Have I stuck to my walk-away price?

Section III

Closing the Sale

Chapter 11
The Compelling Reasons to Close

Now that you know the **7 Immutable Laws of Sales Negotiation**, it's time to move into *closing mode*. In this chapter we'll talk about creating a compelling reason to close that aligns your sales and negotiating process with your buyer's needs.

Compelling Reasons To Close

Many salespeople offer discounts to close deals in order to meet timing requirements set by the seller, not the buyer. This is a bad negotiating technique for several reasons. For example, suppose you offer the buyer a 20% discount to close before the end of the quarter.

1. *Sales is about creating an eager buyer.* By creating an artificial timeline to get a discount for the buyer, you have not created any real value to the buyer. If the buyer was convinced you were the best choice and was ready to choose your offering, you have needlessly given away 20% of your revenue.

2. *If the buyer is not ready to commit to you, you have dropped your pants.* What do you think will happen next? If the buyer eventually decides to choose your solution, will he pay full price? Probably not. What minimum discount will he start with? Probably 20%. When does he know you will discount the most? End of quarter. It is very likely that your buyer will wait until the end of the next quarter and start negotiating with a 20% discount. You will have trained

your buyer to delay his purchase and ask for a larger discount at the end of your quarter. If you give 20% at the end of the quarter, a savvy buyer may wonder just how much you'll be willing to offer at the end of the fiscal year. Again, not a pretty picture. You have just thrown away revenue and increased your sales cycle.

A compelling reason to close would focus on the buyer's needs, such as:

- a financial benefit to the buyer
- a personal benefit to the buyer
- the need to meet the buyer's ideal timeline
- the seller's ability to commit resources to solve the buyer's problem
- the buyer's ability to commit resources
- the ability to have a solution in place to satisfy a compelling event

For example, if your solution saves the buyer $500,000 a month, a compelling reason to close would be:

> "I want to get you in the priority implementation queue so you could start getting the $500,000 monthly benefit as quickly as possible; each week of delay costs you $125,000. What are your thoughts?"

The above example shows how you can utilize your financial analysis to close the deal and shorten the sales cycle, and is an example of using **Immutable Law #2**.

Here are a few other examples of focusing on the buyer's needs to create a compelling reason to close:

- "In order to meet your go-live date of July 15, we need to get you into the implementation queue as quickly as possible. That way we commit our resources to you and ensure that the project is successful and everything is perfect. What are your thoughts?"

- "You mentioned that your sales team meets only once a year at the annual sales meeting and that would be the optimal time to implement this solution. Otherwise the rollout becomes logistically difficult. If we can come to an agreement, we can roll this out at the annual meeting. What are your thoughts?"

- "Once we get the solution in place, you will be able to take weekends off and coach your daughter's soccer games. If we can reach an agreement, we can have a solution in place before the season starts. What are your thoughts?"

Do these reasons to close seem better to the buyer? Does it put the seller in a stronger negotiating position? Will knowing and using these compelling reasons to close improve close rates, shorten the sales cycle, maintain price premiums, and align you better with the buyer's needs? *You bet.*

You can use a multitude of benefits for the buyer to create a compelling reason to close. You can develop your own style. Over time you will develop a handful of compelling reasons to close depending on the type of sales situation in which you are involved. Having a compelling reason to close will refocus your conversations on the value, needs, and time frame of the buyer. It will increase your close rates, reduce your discounting, accelerate your sales velocity, and put you in a strong negotiation position. *Again, offering discounts to close business is a poor idea and violates **Immutable Law #6** (Never Give Without Getting).*

Action Items

Before you go into negotiation, ask yourself if you have accomplished the following:

 Do I know the buyer's compelling reason to close?

☑ Is the compelling reason to close based on my needs or the buyer's needs?

Chapter 12
Elements of a Superlative Sales Effort

In working with numerous sales teams worldwide, we have compiled the elements we believe constitute a superlative sales effort. While you don't have to accomplish all of the elements, we highly recommend that you do. Negotiation success is the result of two key things: a superior sales effort, and a well thought-out and executed negotiation strategy and plan. The weaker your sales effort the geometrically worse your close rates become and the geometrically worse your discounting will become. In other words, you'll be significantly better off making sure you accomplish all of these elements during your sales process. *No amount of negotiation planning can make up for a poor sales effort. A strong sales effort is necessary for a strong negotiation. These are the keys to a superlative sales effort:*

1. **You are the Buyer's #1 Choice.** You must be the Buyer's #1 Choice. If you are not the Buyer's #1 Choice, do not negotiate. Go back and sell better. If you *are* the #1 Choice, you have proven you are the best solution and you should command a price premium.

2. **There is a quantifiable financial justification that has been agreed upon.** During your sales process, you and the buyer must quantify and agree on the financial benefits. If you don't know the financial benefit you have created you will be in a reactive negotiation position and you will be forced to defend your price. If you know the value you create, you can share the value you create

with the buyer and command price premiums. *In every sales effort you should know the benefits you are creating for the buyer.*

3. **You know the business problems solved.** You should know why your buyer needs your particular solution and you should be able to understand the key business issues that will be solved. These should be both the tactical and, more importantly, the strategic business issues that will help your buyer. So, in addition to the tactical reasons to implement or use your solution, you should understand the strategic importance of the solution to the financial buyer.

4. **You know the personal benefits of the solution for each decision maker.** Before I go into negotiation I create a list of all the buyers. For each buyer I write down what his or her business reason is for choosing our solution over our competitors. These are easy to understand—they are the same reasons discussed in big meetings. Next, I write down what the personal agendas might be for choosing our solution. How do the buyers benefit from a personal point of view? Will it help their careers? Will it help them spend more time with their family? How does each buyer personally benefit from your winning the business? No one is going to tell you his personal agenda in a room full of people. These are conversations you have in private, preferably out of the office.

The bigger the sale the more critical one-on-one time is with each decision maker. Don't mistake someone's business agenda for someone's personal agenda. While a buyer's stated business agenda may be to improve operations, his personal interests may or may not be aligned with your winning the business. For example, changing vendors may indicate that the buyer's previous choice was wrong. *Always make sure you know how each decision maker benefits—personally.*

5. **You know that each decision maker is a strong champion.** Though your definition of "champion" may differ, I look for 5 key criteria before I call someone a champion:

- Do I know his business agenda?
- Do I know his personal agenda and how he benefits from choosing my solution?
- Has he told me that he wants me to win the sales opportunity?
- Has he told me about the personal agenda of others? and
- Has he gone out of his way proactively to help me win this sale?

If I can answer yes to all of the above questions, then I know I have a champion. I want all the decision makers to be champions. This ensures a great long-term profitable relationship for both sides. And while it may not be possible to have this kind of relationship with all the decision makers, this is what you want to strive for.

6. **You know the problems and price of taking no action.** You should understand the alternatives of *not* solving the business problem with your solution. What problems will continue? What problems will be exacerbated? What new problems will occur because old ones are not solved? What price will they pay if they don't take action? If the buyer chooses the competitor, what risks will he inherit that he would not inherit with your solution?

7. **You have confirmed that the buyer knows your unique competitive advantages.** You must create separation between you and your competitor. Your prospect should know your unique competitive advantages and how they apply to him and his company. The buyer should be able to tell you what makes you unique and the value it brings to him and his company. It is not enough for you to know your competitive advantages; your buyer must know them, internalize them, and understand how he will be positively affected by those competitive advantages.

8. **You know how to be proactive and you know the budget and decision-making process.** This may seem basic — and it is. It is still necessary, however, to point out because I have noticed many

salespeople are not fully prepared with all the information they need. You need to know the decision-making process in advance. Who controls the budget? How are decisions made? How much is in the budget? Where else can budget come from? And when is the next budgeting cycle? What obstacles might you encounter? You want to be proactive and remove obstacles *before* negotiations. You want to have budget allocated in advance of negotiations.

9. **You know the "ideal go-live" date.** You should know the ideal date to go live or put the solution in place. This creates a compelling reason to move forward and close the sale. Is the buyer's ideal date a hard date? A soft date? Why did he choose that date or time frame? What is unique about it? What will happen if he misses this date? Knowing the go-live date will help create a sense of urgency that will speed the sales cycle and reduce negotiation time. This will allow you to dedicate the correct resources to make the sale a success for your buyer. It will allow you to expand the agreement for both parties by ensuring that the complete solution is in place, and that it is done right the first time according to the buyer's needs.

10. **You have proven you are the least risky solution.** People and companies buy risk, not price. When you have shown you are the least risky solution you become the #1 Choice of your buyer. Risk comes in two varieties: personal risk and business risk. You want to lower both of these risks for the buyer. For a sophisticated buyer it is rarely if ever about price. *It is all about risk.* No one wants to sidetrack his 15-year career and pick a risky vendor just to save the company a few dollars.

In summary

Put yourself in a strong position to negotiate and command price premiums. If you accomplish all these elements of a superlative sales effort during your sales process, you will be in a good position to negotiate. No amount of negotiation strategy can make up for a poor sales effort. A strong sales effort allows you to create value. A strong negotiation plan allows you to build a profitable long-term relationship. If you have put in a strong sales effort, you are now able to create and execute your negotiation plan. A strong sales effort is essential in order to negotiate well.

Chapter 13
International Use of the 7 Immutable Laws

These **7 Immutable Laws** have been successfully used by sales professionals all over the world. The Sales Optimization Group has worked with companies, executives, sales leaders, and salespeople worldwide on six continents, from over more than one hundred countries. These laws have been used in western markets, eastern markets, and emerging markets around the world and have gotten consistently great results. Remarkably, we have not yet encountered any sales professional or executive who has stated that any one of the **Immutable Laws** was not appropriate for his culture or country. If you know of a culture or country where these laws would not apply, please notify us. We are always looking to update our knowledge base.

How to use the 7 Immutable Laws internationally

We encourage you to use these **7 Immutable Laws** on a global basis in every one of your sales negotiations. Using them should help you increase your sales and negotiation success. While the **7 Immutable Laws** themselves will not change with international use, the way you execute the laws may vary.

Consider **Immutable Law #1**: *You must be the Buyer's #1 Choice*. This **Immutable Law** is critical in every single negotiation we have seen throughout the world. With that said, the actions that you use to confirm and verify that you are the Buyer's #1 Choice will vary.

For example, in many parts of the U.S. you could ask very directly, "All things being equal, would we be your #1 Choice?" In other cultures and countries such as Japan and parts of China, you could never be so direct in asking that question. Rather, you would be called upon to confirm that fact in other ways and by asking different questions and then noticing the buyer's response. In either of these countries, however, you still must be the Buyer's #1 Choice; the integrity of *Immutable Law #1* *remains and it doesn't change at all.*

In some cultures your competitive advantage might be that you are the biggest vendor. While that may be a competitive advantage in some cultures, other cultures may put premium value on how long you have been in business rather than your size. In fact, such a claim that you are the biggest vendor might be perceived as a boast and put you at a disadvantage.

The way you execute the **7 Immutable Laws** will vary depending on the culture and country in which you are selling and negotiating. You should tailor your execution of the laws just as you would customize and tailor your sales and negotiation approach depending on the individuals and corporate culture of your buyer.

What does this mean to you?

You can profitably use these **7 Immutable Laws** on a global basis. As a great salesperson and negotiator, you will tailor the execution of these laws to meet the culture of the companies, individuals, and countries where you are selling. Use these **7 Immutable Laws** to get your full asking price, create more valuable agreements, improve your close rates, accelerate your sales velocity, increase the lifetime value of your buyers, *and* create more satisfied customers and clients.

Chapter 14
The 7 Steps Guide: Executing Your Negotiation Plan

Putting together your negotiation plan

When you are ready to begin negotiation, put together your negotiation plan. Here is our *7 Steps Guide* which completely matches and dovetails with our **7 Immutable Laws**. You can close on any step—the sooner the better.

STEP #1 You Must Be the Buyer's #1 Choice.

WHY THIS LAW IS IMPORTANT

You cannot discount your way to the #1 place. You must be the **Buyer's #1 Choice** before you begin to negotiate. If you are not the **Buyer's #1 Choice**, the buyer is using you and negotiating with you to beat down the real winner's price. If you *are* the number one choice, it is because you have put in a superior sales effort and proven that you are the best solution; therefore, you should command a price premium. *Never enter into a negotiation without knowing you are the **Buyer's #1 Choice**.*

ACTION ITEMS

- ☑ Have I put in a superlative sales effort?
- ☑ Have I confirmed I am the **Buyer's #1 Choice**?
- ☑ If I am the **Buyer's #1 Choice**, it's time to start executing my negotiation plan.
- ☑ If I am not the **Buyer's #1 Choice**, I need to go back and sell better.

STEP #2 You Must Know the Financial Benefit Your Solution Creates

WHY THIS LAW IS IMPORTANT

If you don't know the financial benefit your solution provides, you will find yourself forced into a reactive negotiation position and you will be forced to defend your price rather than focus the negotiation on the value your solution provides. On the other hand, if you know the financial benefit you create, you also create a compelling reason to close and shorten the sales cycle.

ACTION ITEMS

- ☑ Do I know the financial value my solution provides to my buyer?
- ☑ Have I co-authored and agreed upon the benefit with the buyer?
- ☑ Do I know the monthly benefit?
- ☑ Do I know the annual benefit?
- ☑ Bonus points if I can relate those benefits to the change in market valuation.

STEP #3 Anticipate Getting Squeezed On Price

WHY THIS LAW IS IMPORTANT

Price negotiation is not cost justification. If you are the Buyer's #1 Choice, your buyer wants to buy from you. The next question is, "What is the lowest price I can get it for?" Buyers will try to squeeze you on price. You must be prepared to resist squeezes by refocusing the conversation on the benefits of your solution. By refocusing on the benefits of the solution, you are giving a polite "no" to their request for a discount and offering them a face-saving way to agree to the sale.

ACTION ITEMS

- ☑ Am I prepared to recognize and identify squeezes?
- ☑ Have I prepared a list of 7 ways to respond to squeezes by giving a polite "no" and by refocusing the conversation on the benefits of my solution?
- ☑ Am I prepared to be the dry towel?

STEP #4 Be Proactive on Budget and Remove Decision Making Obstacles in Advance

WHY THIS LAW IS IMPORTANT

If you don't know the budget and decision-making process, you are likely to have to cut price to fit in "this year's budget" and/or get beat up along the path completing the sale. If you know the budget and decision-making process, you can proactively remove obstacles that you may encounter and proactively get budget allocated from the current budget and future budgets so that you can command price premiums and get your full asking price—or better.

ACTION ITEMS

 Do I know:
- The buyer's current budget?
- Who controls the budget and how decisions are made?
- Where else budget can come from?
- When the next budgeting cycle is?
- What obstacles can get in the way?

☑ Have I proactively:
- Gotten budget allocated for this year and future years' budgets?
- Addressed and managed any obstacles that may arise with the purchasing process?

STEP #5 Expand the Pie with a Set of Non-Monetary Trade-Ups

WHY THIS LAW IS IMPORTANT

You have the opportunity to increase the value you deliver to your buyer and at the same time create more value for yourself as well. You can do this and still maintain a price premium by creating a set of non-monetary trade-ups.

ACTION ITEMS

☑ Have I created a list of "non-monetary gives" that are high value to the buyer and low cost to me?

☑ Have I created a list of "gets" that are high value to me and low cost to the buyer?

☑ Based on the two lists, have I created a set of non-monetary trade-ups that will expand the pie?

☑ Over time, am I looking to develop a standardized set or bundles of trade-ups?

STEP #6 Never Give Without Getting

WHY THIS LAW IS IMPORTANT

"Never give without getting" is a fundamental of negotiation. If you give without getting the buyer will perceive that "give" to have little value and it will have set you up for future discounting with the buyer on future sales opportunities—as well as encourage him to ask for more discounts on this sale.

ACTION ITEMS

☑ Have I created a monetary trade-off chain of "gives" and "gets"?

☑ Have I reviewed my monetary trade-off chain; have I explored where I can substitute non-monetary "gives" for discounts?

☑ Have I gone back and reviewed Immutable Laws #1 through #5... before I give any discount?

☑ Have I changed my belief system on discounting and watched the positive results?

STEP #7 Know Your Walk-Away Price and Conditions

WHY THIS LAW IS IMPORTANT

When you are prepared to walk away, the buyer knows he has gotten all he can out of you. It also allows the buyer to rethink his position and consider the poor alternatives which may occur by not completing a sale with you.

ACTION ITEMS

☑ Do I know my walk-away price and condition before I enter into negotiation?

☑ Do I know how to politely walk away?

☑ Have I remembered that walking away will strengthen my position?

☑ Have I stuck to my walk-away price?

Chapter 15
Using the Closing Time Quick Sheet™

On the following page, you will see our **Closing Time Quick Sheet™**, which many of our clients use to implement our system. Please feel free to try it on a deal or two. If you find it useful, you may want to license this and our other sales negotiation materials. The payback on the Quick Sheet is usually enormous and it could be a great investment for you. Take the profit you make by using our Quick Sheet™ and invest it in licensing our suite of training materials and services. We grant you the right to use this on up to two (2) sales opportunities. When you combine our training with our tools and ongoing reinforcement, you will maximize the use of our system and geometrically increase your sales and negotiation success.

To enable your two-time use of the Quick Sheet™, please visit our website at **www.ClosingTimeTraining.com/QuickSheet.php**. You can also download a bigger version of the Quick Sheet.

If you are interested in training or licensing our Quick Sheet™ for more than two uses, please call us at **866.Sales.06**.

Closing Time:
The 7 Immutable Laws of Sales Negotiation
Quick Sheet™

- **You Must Be the Buyer's #1 Choice.**
  Are we the buyer's #1 choice? _____
  Why?_____

- **You Must Know The Financial Benefit Your Solution Creates**
  What is the Payback/Financial Benefit?_____

- **Anticipate Getting Squeezed on Price.**
  Refocus on Value Delivered/Benefit to the Prospect (multiple times)
  Stand 1:_____
  Stand 2:_____
  Stand 3:_____
  Stand 4:_____
  Stand 5:_____
  What makes us the least risky solution?_____

- **Be Proactive on Budget and Remove Decision Making Obstacles in Advance**
  How much is in the budget? _____
  Who controls it? _____
  When is the next budget cycle? _____
  Where else can budget come from?_____
  Have we removed all purchasing obstacles?_____

- **Expand the Pie with a Set of Non-Monetary Trade-Ups:**

GIVE	GET
Extra People at Training	PO Today, Extra years on contract
Priority Implementation	
60 Day Payment Terms	

- **Never Give without Getting : Create a $ Trade-Off Chain**

GIVE	GET
0-5% discount	
0-10% discount	
0-15% discount	

- **Know your walk away price.** That signals to the prospect that you cannot give any
  more and they have gotten the best price.
  What is our walk away price? _____
  How will we politely walk away? _____

- **Compelling Reason to Close:** _____

Chapter 16
Closing Time

I want to thank you for your investment in this book. I am grateful for and honored by your time and attention. As I mentioned before, when you "close a sale" you are really creating a new beginning. With this goal in mind, I would be honored in pursuing such an ongoing relationship with each of you. The Sales Optimization Group offers a portfolio of sales and negotiation solutions to corporations, businesses, and sales professionals. We have a number of products and services that are sure to help you to accelerate your sales and increase your negotiation success.

If you are an investor, executive, CEO, VP of sales or in sales management, some logical next steps would be to:

- train your team with our customized on-site training;
- invite us to speak at your next sales conference;
- leverage our customized web-based training;
- license our tools and methodology;
- embed our training and methodology into your CRM systems.

If you are a salesperson, some logical next steps would be to:

- take our online mini-course;
- take our online training full course;
- take our live training classes and become Platinum Certified.

(Note: Platinum Certification is one of the key qualifications many top organizations are looking for in sales reps and is rapidly becoming an industry standard. It will also help you close more sales, earn more commissions, and free up personal time.)

You can learn more information about our solutions by visiting our website at **www.ClosingTimeTraining.com** or calling us at **866-Sales-66**.

Thank you again for selecting and reading *Closing Time: The 7 Immutable Laws of Sales Negotiation*. I look forward to a long and lasting relationship.

Ron Hubsher
CEO
Sales Optimization Group

Thank you for investing your time in this book.

If you want, please download our bonus chapter at
www.ClosingTimeBook.com

Want to get your team trained?

Our customized training programs range from 1 hour to 1 day. Payback is usually achieved in a matter of days.

We serve clients worldwide.

If you would like to get your team trained, please call us at:

650-520-9849